How Things Happen

a guide for regular people

by

Bill Kane

To Michael.
Mine well.
Bill Kane
3/10

rp

Published by

rp communications LLC
Westwood, New Jersey 07675

regular people

I write this for those I call regular people. regular people come in all skin tones and ethnic backgrounds. They are of all political persuasions. They practice all religions. They are of all genders and sexual preferences, all economic strata, and live in all geographic locations.

regular people are those who go about their daily lives trying to be the best they can be without trying to hurt anyone in any fashion, or using their energy for less than honorable purposes. They are not phonies, crooks, or greedy people. They are not plastic people who don't stand for or care about anything.

regular people simply want to live their lives in the best way they can, caring about humanity and the planet, and wanting to be unbothered and respected.

This is for them.

∞∞∞∞∞∞∞∞∞∞∞∞∞∞∞∞∞∞∞∞

Acknowledgments

If Julie did not speak, the source would not have been remembered. If Ray had not listened, not a word would have been written. If Bob and Mary Ellen had not read, there would not have been a second draft. If Elisa had not listened, read, and talked, the transition could not have been made. If Darlene and Marissa were not patient and loving, there would be nothing to acknowledge.

I thank them all and everyone else who was involved in the process of crafting this book, but most of all I thank the Creator for giving me the assignment.

Contents

regular people   iii

Acknowledgments   v

Preface   3

Introduction.   9

Why we think as we do   17

The Ingredients **27**

The Sciences **31**

Quantum Physics.   33

Morphic Resonance   39

Chaos Mathematics   45

The Technology **53**

The Human Body   55

The Tools **61**

Thoughts   65

Emotions   69

Feelings   73

Beliefs.   79

Allowing.   83

Intentions.   87

Energy   91

Other Things **95**

Ego   99

Practice   103

Presence   107

What we may be **111**

About the Author   123

Afterthoughts

Barometric Pressure 7

The Heresy of a Gentle Man 15

Some Time. 25

Human Creation 37

Smiling for Eden 43

Effect as Cause 51

Technology 101 59

Moods 67

Emotions 71

Feelings 77

Believe 81

Allowing. 85

Small Change 89

Vibration 93

Humble Gods 101

Shaky Addition 105

Now. 109

Metamorphosis 121

"If the doors of perception were cleansed, everything would appear to man as it is, infinite."

William Blake, Poet

Preface

What you are about to read is the result of a lifetime of watching people and events and wondering why people do what they do and how things happen as they do. Why do people fly planes into buildings? Why do populations get hyped up about war or some other adrenalin producing event only to change their enthusiasm after a time? Why is the human race repeating the same cycles of violence, destruction, and greed while everyone decries these shortcomings year after year after year, since the beginning of human interaction?

On a more mundane level, why do people dismiss anything that puts their thinking outside of their comfort zone of "that's what we have always believed," or "this is how we always do it"?

I have spent most of my adult life satisfying a reading obsession with a study of human potential. That study has led me to the conclusions that follow. What you will find here is how things happen. All things.

Don't be put off by the enormity of the claim that this is how all things happen. I too was shocked that I had the audacity to make the claim. What I didn't realize is that it is not that complicated. You do not have to be a rocket scientist, or a guru, or a genius to understand this. You simply have to relax and allow yourself to be a human being and you will know this is true.

∞∞∞∞∞∞∞∞∞∞∞∞∞∞∞∞∞∞∞∞

This little book will give you information that may be new to you about how things happen in this world, which means your consciousness about human existence and potential will be higher than before. What you choose to do afterward is, of course, up to you. That's the beauty of free will.

Many will read this and think it nice and then continue their lives in the same fashion, letting circumstances and others have too much influence over the reality in which they live.

Some will become energized into understanding our lives are in our control and we are on a journey to recover the knowledge and skills we as humans possess and are entitled to exercise.

I hope you continue the journey.

∞∞∞∞∞∞∞∞∞∞∞∞∞∞∞∞∞∞∞∞

The way things happen are a combination of spiritual and material interactions utilizing a set of what I like to call *ingredients*. There are eleven ingredients, all of which you already possess. What follows is a simple guide to help you understand those ingredients.

Any process used to construct your world, any method you choose, I call your *recipe*. I use the terms *ingredients* and *recipe* because every view of reality is a personal artistic creation. Every person using the same ingredients will create a separate recipe, a separate reality. Recipes are personal creations.

If you found yourself in a war zone or you found yourself at a romantic dinner with your true love, you may ask, "How did I get here? What made this happen?" A whole lot of recipes, yours and others, got you to where you are right now.

Religions, philosophies, stardom, vegetarianism, capitalism, loving kindness, terrorism, soccermomism, militarism, and the routine of farming are but a few of the recipes people use to create their own world. There are billions more. Humans have recipes for all levels of their existence. Bias of any kind needs a recipe, as does anything else that occurs, like falling in love.

Patriotism is a recipe, as are treachery and loyalty. Being a bully cannot be done without a bully recipe; likewise for the bully's victim.

Congeniality, gruffness, cynicism, or any type of demeanor requires a recipe of the things found here.

Most people have thousands of recipes they follow. Some recipes are created and utilized in a very deliberate manner. Most, more haphazardly and silently accepted. Some are designed outside of our individual consciousness and accepted as the norm for our individuality.

If we allow our recipes to be created by others, we live our lives by the dictates of others. Unfortunately, the enthusiasm and fervor of those who are misguided about the concept of self-interest has been stronger than the rest of us. This has brought us war, starvation, and terrorism, to name a few problems of the planet directly attributed to human thought.

Big things that happen on the planet are usually the result of a great collection of humans following the same recipe. Those collective outcomes can only come about by people making individual decisions.

Knowing what makes things happen in the world is not a special privilege. There are no magical talents needed to understand these things. There are no educational requirements. Every human being is an integral part of the process of making things happen. Most people however, never give it much thought.

We are, in fact, making things happen every second of every day we exist. We shape our world. According to all the great teachings, we can learn to do so consciously. We as humans are not here just for the ride, we are in charge. Our reality is created by ourselves.

Your religious beliefs are not compromised by understanding this. Any sense of scientific predominance in your thinking also need not be challenged.

As you will see, we can be much more than we have ever dreamt. We can be like the best who ever walked the earth.

This is how I see things happen. I hope you will benefit from these words. I hope you will remember miracles.

∞∞∞∞∞∞∞∞∞∞∞∞∞∞∞∞∞∞

Barometric Pressure

Let us pretend we are in charge.
Remember that?

Let us imagine for an instant we are in a magical place.
If enough of us did, we would be.

Let us bring some order to the use of this new skill.
Everybody calm down.

Now, think. . . . **normal weather**

∞∞∞∞∞∞∞∞∞∞∞∞∞∞∞∞∞∞∞∞∞∞

Introduction

What makes the events in our lives happen as they do? How are new things created? What about our feelings toward someone or a group of people? How does that process begin? What information do we use to make a decision? Where do we get it? What are the rules that must be followed to allow joy to be brought into our lives? How about all this bad stuff that has happened to us? What brought it about? How about natural phenomena? What causes a hurricane? A snow storm? How does a heart attack happen?

Pick anything you would like—war, poverty, wealth creation, illness, music, a dog fetching a ball, a hug. They all happen as a result of the same things. Even if you are sitting there reading this thinking, "this is nonsense," what is the process that made you think that? What did you feel? Did a memory get triggered? Has a chemical reaction occurred that caused you to be negative? Or do you simply believe this is nonsense?

Are you allowing new information to enter your worldview or paradigm? Or are you using a closed mind recipe? Are you wise enough to suspend your beliefs while you evaluate this information?

The ingredients that make things happen consist of three sciences, one piece of technology, and seven tools.

The three sciences, Quantum Physics, Morphic Resonance, and Chaos Mathematics will someday make a leap into the forefront of our thinking. These sciences will eventually be developed to the point where they are a part of the everyday consciousness of humanity.

Quantum Physics, among other things, describes the process whereby all things physical come into existence.

Morphic Resonance is the gateway to understanding karma or predestination or whatever you choose to call the things we seem to be destined to experience and live. It is the process whereby information comes from the field. It is how a bird knows to migrate. It is how any species gets its "mysterious" information.

Chaos Mathematics dazzles us with visual effects while educating us about the concept of cause and effect to the nth degree, incorporating innumerable variables. It shows how the smallest effort placed in precisely the right place can bring about massive change. A butterfly flapping its wings can actually cause a tornado. It is the mathematics of dynamical systems.

Chaos Mathematics also talks about attractors, which draw things into the future rather than relying on our traditional understanding of cause and effect as the basis for development. Fractal geometry, derived from Chaos Mathematics, has already shown us shifts to other dimensions.

These are the sciences that make things happen. Of course most of the old rules still apply. Newtonian or Classical Physics still applies, but these new sciences have taken us to a deeper understanding of how things happen. Most people have never heard of them. In fact most people working in the scientific community have no clue how these work. These three sciences are the primary scientific responses to the use of our technology and our tools.

Don't worry; you don't have to know much about these, only that they are in operation. Very few people really understand the process of creation that gives a rose its beauty, or the chemistry of its fragrance, but most enjoy both of these gifts. These sciences are like that. There is no need to know the intricacies of how they work, only that they do. Each of the other ingredients puts them into operation constantly. It is happening right now as you read this.

∞∞∞∞∞∞∞∞∞∞∞∞∞∞∞∞∞∞∞∞

The greatest piece of technology we possess is the **human body**. It is with this technology that we enable our physical existence. Most of us simply go along inside our bodies on autopilot, not knowing we can really have an adventure if we learn how to use these things. Our bodies are designed for the activity of creation. Not just to preserve the species, but to create everything. Most people live and die without ever understanding this.

The tools we use to activate our technology are **thoughts, emotions, feelings, beliefs, intentions, the ability to allow,** and the **energy** of the universe. It is the mastery of these tools that will lead you to finding your true self and an understanding of your power.

The ingredients listed here, the sciences, the body, and the tools, in various combinations, create the processes by which everything we experience happens.

It really is that simple.

How dare you! You may cry. . . . . Who do you think you are? How can you possibly claim to know how things happen? What is this miracle nonsense? What arrogance. Has your cheese completely fallen off its crackers?

Everyone knows God makes everything happen. **He** will do as **He** wishes!

Or

Everyone knows there is no god. All things happen due to cause and effect on the material plane, which is the only thing that actually exists.

Or

Everyone knows that science has proven that all matter is energy and that time is really constructed by our imagination. What we think is reality is actually an illusion.

Or

Everyone I know would think you are nuts and be leaving right about here . . . . Bye.

Which *everyone* are you a part of? There are many more.

Our view of our existence and power as human beings is very diverse. We have about as many ideas of who we are as we have cultures and religions. The fact is, we have yet to scratch the surface of the potential we have as human beings. The truth, in my understanding, knows no doctrine or dogma. So be sure, this is not a book about religion or any ideology.

What does it mean when I say things happen by the principles of these ingredients?

I mean, whatever occurs in the world, occurs in line with or as a result of the principles laid out in these sciences. Our mastery of the tools as applied to the flow of energy through our bodies and to the extra-physical skills we can develop provides the theater for these sciences to perform. Combined, the processes discovered by these relatively new sciences are what shape the universe.

Just think about that for a second. The sciences by which everything happens in the universe have only been in the minds of mankind for about 100 years in the case of Quantum Physics, and less than 50 for Morphic Resonance and the Chaos theory of mathematics.

∞∞∞∞∞∞∞∞∞∞∞∞∞∞∞∞∞∞∞

Try to set aside your normal prejudices and practicalities while you read this. You will not turn into a demon or even a frog for reading it, nor will it cause you to join a convent. What you read here will, however, change your view of the world, if you are willing to think outside the box. If enough of us think outside the box, we can change the box.

∞∞∞∞∞∞∞∞∞∞∞∞∞∞∞∞∞∞∞

The sciences are the link to other dimensions. Our view of reality is constantly being shaped by these ingredients. We can consciously change how we perceive things, which will change our world.

If our spirits are here to learn and become complete, or to be reunited with God as most believe, then we must look at the possibility that our view of the world needs an update. Our paradigm may be outdated.

It is as if we were running our computer with Windows 3.1 as our operating system. That system was replaced by at least four upgrades over the past few years.

We are a few versions behind in operating the human experience. Our manner of viewing ourselves and our world will change just by knowing this, but you can do much better.

Let's upgrade. Our concepts of how we perceive God, our understanding of who we are, and our ideas about how the physical plane functions, are all subject to an upgrade.

All the great religions and spiritual teachings have told us we are more than just our bodies and our minds and our emotions. Most tell us we are part of the infinite, part of the divine. All tell us we can at least have access to divine intervention if we behave in the proper manner. We are part of the One. This is what we are taught. Everywhere.

Even if you are not religious and don't believe in anything taught by religions, according to science, you still are part of the one. Like it or not.

Of course we have also been led to believe that it takes complete dedication and sacrifice beyond what most of us are willing to make in order to experience this divine nature that is ours. We must live the life of the ascetic. We must become as saints. So we have been told. Those things are no longer true. You do not have to live in a cave or a monastery to be in touch with the divine.

I hope to help you understand this by beginning with some history and then giving a brief explanation of the three sciences. We will then spend some time looking at the different ways the diversity of culture has formed our thinking about our bodies. The human body is designed to be tuned to other dimensions. Right now only a few ever get to that level of perfection. We need more.

We will look at the tools we have available within our bodies and minds to make best use of our technology. What are our emotions, our feelings, our thoughts, and the other tools? What do they have to do with fulfilling our potential? Do these things interact scientifically or is this all just hocus-pocus? What is our role in creation? Do we have one? Is it minor or are we major players in the creation process?

You may be left wanting more as you read about the various ingredients. I hope so. This is a guide. It is specifically written to increase your desire for more knowledge.

There are many places to find more information on each of the subjects covered here.

∞∞∞∞∞∞∞∞∞∞∞∞∞∞∞∞∞∞∞

The Heresy of a Gentle Man

Love is the highest vibrational energy human beings can attain.

It is the closest we can get to the ultimate vibration of perfect harmony.

The higher the vibration, the more loving the manifestation.

Love brings love quickly.
This is how science will prove God is Love.

Then we can all do the wine trick!

∞∞∞∞∞∞∞∞∞∞∞∞∞∞∞∞∞∞∞∞∞

Why we think as we do

"If you would understand anything, observe its beginning and its development."

Aristotle, Philosopher

Our thinking on a lot of things has gone through radical shifts over the centuries. What we think and believe is how the reality we live is created. During the time of the Roman Empire, for example, people believed in a whole lot of different Gods. There was a God who was worshiped for just about anything you could think of. There were Gods of war, Gods of harvest, Gods of love, and Gods of wealth. You name it; the Romans had a God for it.

Where did they all go? One day the Roman Empire is ruling the Western world and their Gods are the most revered, or at least feared. The next day—well not exactly the next day—all gone. One God, the Christian God, is officially worshipped.

How did that happen? You might say it was the will of God enlightening the world to the divinity of Jesus Christ, or you might say it was a political compromise on the part of Emperor Constantine to preserve the Roman Empire. Perhaps both of those reasons and more are the cause; however, what came after is relevant here.

Once the Christian religion took hold as the official state religion of the Roman Empire, the entire Western culture was transformed. I am not picking on Christianity here, I am looking at history. I use this as an example to illustrate the power of accepted beliefs on a large scale. I don't believe any single concept has had a more profound effect on Western culture than the acceptance of Christianity as the state religion by the Romans. From that time on the entire Western civilization, indeed the world, was changed.

After the fall of Rome in the fifth century, the Western world went into a kind of slump intellectually and culturally. The Roman Catholic

Church became the glue holding society together, and the Church didn't provide for nor allow the dissemination of much new information to regular people. Very few people could read or write. Science was almost non-existent. The Church became more and more influential in society until it literally ran all of the political institutions in Europe.

The Church was pretty paranoid and superstitious. The fact is, people were held back and the entire society and culture was fear based, mainly from a very conservative Christian perspective. For example, the use of the concept and the number zero was forbidden until the sixteenth century. This was because zero could be interpreted as being infinite, and only God could be called that. That behavior may seem silly to most by today's standards, but it is true. The accountants must have been very good.

Remember Copernicus? He figured out that the earth was not the center of the universe, and in fact, the earth revolved around the sun instead of the other way around. The Church taught the opposite. Many think Copernicus didn't publish this information until he was near death for fear of reprisal from the Church.

The Church didn't care for people messing with its dogma. More than a few people were imprisoned or killed for expressing belief in Copernican theories. The great astronomer Galileo was thrown into jail and philosopher Giordano Bruno was burned at the stake. That was only about 500 years ago.

Today we look at that kind of thinking as if it were infantile and stupid. But remember, the entire Western society thought that way. Science was controlled by Christianity, as was the entire Western culture. Our view of the world and beyond was formed by this behavior. Even though other ideologies and religions existed, it was Christianity that ruled Western society. Christianity did some very weird things over the centuries, as all religions seem to do when their turf is threatened. All the lunacy aside, they still brought the teachings of Jesus Christ into the human consciousness. Much good was accomplished as a result. If the knowledge of Jesus was unknown, the world would be a very, very different place.

∞∞∞∞∞∞∞∞∞∞∞∞∞∞∞∞∞∞∞∞∞

In Europe, and later America, our scientific knowledge didn't begin to flourish until the Renaissance period beginning in the fifteenth century. The most famous and perhaps the most brilliant scientist was Isaac Newton, who was born in 1643. It was Newton and his contemporaries who created what we call Classical or Newtonian Physics.

Classical Physics relies on the mechanistic, cause-and-effect system of scientific inquiry. It was with Classical Physics that many of our discoveries were made, allowing us to create the modern world. Classical Physics predominates the thinking in the scientific community until this day. It is the scientific thought that most people understand. In Classical Physics everything is cut and dried. The universe is considered to be like a big machine. When you push here, something happens over there. When you turn this, it causes that to happen. It is very tidy and concise. It is very systematic and neatly constructed. Everything has its place and everything behaves as it is supposed to. What goes up must come down, et cetera. It still works and it is still true.

Classical Physics is the science that ruled our world for about 300 years. It became so ingrained in our thinking that the science that came after is having a hard time finding its way into the culture.

∞∞∞∞∞∞∞∞∞∞∞∞∞∞∞∞∞∞∞

During the latter part of the nineteenth and early part of the twentieth centuries, scientists made major breakthroughs that changed everything once again. Physicists were looking at matter on smaller and smaller scales.

In the first part of the twentieth century, Albert Einstein's famous theory of relativity came up with the equation $e = mc^2$. What that really means is that energy and matter are the same thing. That was about 100 years ago. What Einstein did was set the scientific world on its head.

For centuries it was an acceptable fact that matter was in fact solid and concrete. We knew that a thing was a thing. A shoe was a shoe. Big things were usually made from small things, but everything was a solid piece of matter of some kind. Just the way most people think today.

But none of that is true. Well, it is true, but something else is true at a different level.

The rules of Classical Physics don't necessarily disappear because something else was discovered. A shoe is still a shoe, and it is made of matter just as it was before Einstein. There is something new, however, that Einstein proved. That shoe, when you break it down to its smallest bit of matter, can be broken down even further and further until we find that even the atoms and the electrons making up the atoms of the shoe are not as they appear to be. Everything is, in fact, energy. And it is always moving. The really amazing thing is that it is not only always moving, but it is constantly coming into and out of existence. It appears and disappears constantly.

Think about that. According to Albert Einstein and the scientific community, everything you see before your eyes, including yourself, is made of the same stuff and is blinking in and out of existence on a consistent basis.

Einstein also showed that time is relative. So when you are waiting for something good to happen and time seems to be dragging, it really is dragging. It is relative to the point of view of the person considering it. Science, in fact, has shown that time actually doesn't exist. There is no future and there is no past. There is only now. And if that's true, then why don't we live our lives in a timeless fashion? What would it be like if we did?

In some respects we have come full circle on the time thing. My guess is, humans didn't consider the concept of time very much early on. It probably caught on as a way of thinking when we started planting things on a regular basis. We would have to consider time to figure out when the harvest was due. Cavemen didn't punch a time clock or go bananas over a fancy wristwatch. Just think for a moment what your life would be like if your brain never learned the concept of time. Watch a two-year-old; you will see how free we were.

∞∞∞∞∞∞∞∞∞∞∞∞∞∞∞∞∞∞∞

Scientific discoveries have changed the way people view their existence here on earth. Consider the paradigm shift when the first person figured out what fire could do. In more modern times, consider the invention of the automobile, the airplane, the television, or the telephone. We certainly have come to think differently since these things entered our lives.

Most recently, the computer and its access to unlimited information have been introduced to the world. Think about the ramifications of these changes down the road. As I write this, obviously there are things that pop up that I don't know about. Years ago only learned scholars could do this kind of work. Now someone like me can stop what I'm doing and use the built-in research feature of my word processing software. It is connected online to vast research databases allowing me to gather the information I need. In a few minutes I'm back on track. That may have taken months just a few short years ago.

Right now we are in a kind of Limbo, a place in between. Our world is being bombarded with inventions based on the new sciences of the last 70 to 100 years, but our societal structure and our cultural thinking is still back there in the seventeenth century with Isaac Newton.

∞∞∞∞∞∞∞∞∞∞∞∞∞∞∞∞∞∞∞∞

In the East, too, we saw shifts in the way people saw their world. One man sat under a tree and became the Buddha, and the entire continent of Asia was changed.

While many in the West were living in the Dark Ages and using their energy to prevent their souls from being captured by the devil, people in Asia were using intuitive knowledge to heal and to understand energy flow in our bodies. Most of that kind of activity was forbidden as evil or witchcraft by the Western church and society. The Asians were looking at other things in the metaphysical world for a long time with great understanding.

Acupuncture, acupressure, and other energy techniques were in use thousands of years ago in Asian countries. The meridian system is a system of over three hundred little vortices where energy comes into and out of your body. There are at least seven large vortices in your body called Chakras that are studied by many cultures in the East.

There are various art forms that teach about the flow of energy. It is amazing that today with our scientific technology we are beginning to prove things that people knew thousands of years ago when there was no chance of scientific proof. Science of the West is beginning to validate the knowledge of the East. We are finding out that many of the arts of the East have a valid scientific structure.

There were also people in the West discovering an understanding of energy and some of the methods of its flow through the human body. Unfortunately, these teachings were mostly hidden and not as openly developed as in the East. The oppression of the people in charge kept them from flourishing and reaching the mainstream.

∞∞∞∞∞∞∞∞∞∞∞∞∞∞∞∞∞∞∞∞

The main point about the history of our thinking is that we tend to get stuck in certain ruts for a long time until something moves us along. There is no positive need fulfilled or useful gain received from judging history. Acknowledging history, learning from it, and going from there is the route to progress.

If you really think about it, as much as we have advanced since the biblical days, we really haven't come very far. Of course we have come far in the advancement of technology and science to conquer the physical plane. Our discoveries have been fantastic in the area of how we deal with physical matter. We can go to the moon. We can build huge buildings and monuments. We can fly. And we can kill with a proficiency never dreamed of by ancient humankind. But we have yet to really understand ourselves.

Many are still of the mindset where if someone is not behaving in a way they think proper, they must be possessed by the devil. It wasn't too long ago in human history that those people would have been burned at the stake. Even today some would like to continue that behavior. Others are still of the mindset that anything called spiritual must be considered part of the conspiracy to keep humans subservient to those who wish to hog the material wealth of the planet.

∞∞∞∞∞∞∞∞∞∞∞∞∞∞∞∞∞∞∞∞

So far we have looked at some things that have shaped the thinking of humanity and helped bring about the reality we live. Our view of things is important in how that reality is created.

Right now you may be thinking "sure our cultures are created by our worldview, but you said everything in the universe. How about the natural stuff? The stars, the trees, the water, the earth? We don't make them happen!"

Ah, but we do. All things in existence happen as a result of the eleven ingredients. You, of course, probably do not believe this, but let me remind you of something. Not long ago your ancestors were told the world was round. They were also told at a later date that human beings could fly. Most people didn't believe either of those statements. Change your worldview, and you change your world.

There are periods in history where the thinking of humankind took great leaps and much of our old thinking became obsolete. I believe the early part of the twenty-first century is one of those times. Humanity is leaving its childhood.

∞∞∞∞∞∞∞∞∞∞∞∞∞∞∞∞∞∞∞

Some Time

Time is running out.
How could that be when it doesn't exist?

Time heals all wounds.
It is really cool when you speed it up.

There's no time like the present.
You got that right.

Thanks for your time.

∞∞∞∞∞∞∞∞∞∞∞∞∞∞∞∞∞∞∞

The Ingredients

The ingredients of how things happen consist of three sciences—**Quantum Physics, Morphic Resonance**, and **Chaos Mathematics**. One piece of technology—the **Human Body**. And seven tools—**Thoughts, Emotions, Feelings, Beliefs, Intentions, Allowing**, and **Energy**.

These ingredients are contained in every recipe you could use to design, direct, or analyze reality. It doesn't make a difference if you choose a religion like Catholicism, Hinduism, or any other religion. It makes no difference if you choose to create your world through a scientific perspective. You could look at things from a metaphysical point of view, or you could operate on autopilot and not give it any thought whatsoever.

Whatever your way of looking at the world, these are the ingredients of the recipes you choose. The sciences work whether you know about them or not. Understanding them will make an enormous difference in what your world will be.

The ignorance of the technology that is the human body is probably the greatest sin of omission committed by the majority of human societies throughout history. That omission can be rectified with an understanding of the tools used to make things happen. Each individual can access and perfect them. When you do, your technology will make the sciences work for you in whatever recipe you choose.

Many people will stop reading this book right about here because it clearly is not providing what they think of as the magic bullet for instant enlightenment, massive riches, or immediate avatar status. Sorry, no recipes here, this is the book of ingredients.

The secret to this book is to read it all the way through even if you find it boring. I am aware this is not a spellbinding page turner that you can't put down. It is simply a list with short definitions and an invitation to think a little differently than before. If you get through it, your life will change because it will connect things you already knew in a way that may be new. This alone will create in your mind a desire for more knowledge.

This alone will put the ingredients to work for you in a way that was not done before. This information can change your life.

Once you know these things, if you are the slightest bit curious or the least bit interested in advancing as a human being, you will want more information. You will begin to think about the recipes that run your life. When you do that, you may attempt to change them. That is when you will take a greater interest in the use of the tools.

We have all heard of the tools. Many recipes teach about the use of the tools. Most people also know there is some sort of science at work in sustaining our existence.

Not enough people understand the importance of the body in applying the tools and causing the sciences to work as we would like. The body is the key. It is the bridge between the physical and the non-physical. When we have a body that is a clear energy conduit, the sciences are ours to command. We create that energy conduit with the same thing we create everything else in our lives. We create it with the tools.

But first we will look at the sciences. What amazes me most about the sciences is that the scientists don't know for sure what is happening. How can the rest of us be so sure about our certainty of knowing how things happen? Because everything is a combination of things. Pure scientific inquiry is obsolete when trying to determine human existence. There must be a coalescence of the material and the spiritual to understand this.

Read on, you may find the answers you have been looking for.

∞∞∞∞∞∞∞∞∞∞∞∞∞∞∞∞∞∞∞∞

The Sciences

Quantum Physics

"Anyone who is not shocked by quantum theory has not understood it."

Niels Bohr, Physicist

Science took a turn inward during the latter part of the nineteenth century and began studying smaller and smaller bits of matter. The scientists were discovering that the tried and true foundations of Classical Physics didn't work on the small particles. Some things didn't fit into the neat classical model.

A new field of study was begun in the late 1800s. A field of study unlike any other. This field of study would affect all the other sciences. It is still incomplete and may never be complete because this science is the study of the interface of our material world and the void or the field or whatever you wish to call the nothingness that is not material. A science was created that studies how things appear out of thin air. It is called Quantum Physics. It sounds crazy, almost magical or miraculous, but it brought us things like television, digital electronic devices, and nanotechnology. It also brought us the atom bomb.

Some of the people who discovered this field of science say that nobody really understands it. Even today there is no agreement on the total theory. That is true because Quantum Physics is the bridge between the physical and the spiritual. It seems to take a little bit of human thought, adds a bit of collapsed waveform and ta-da—we have material reality. It takes human thought and produces what that thought intends. That is my view of Quantum Physics, and as outlandish as it seems, many physicists believe the same.

If you ask your local physicist, you will be told there are at least eight concepts of reality theorized by the various schools of thought in the field. Each concept believes, however, that matter is in fact in the form of waves when it is not being measured. It then only becomes matter when we pay attention. This sounds very strange, but it is a scientific fact.

∞∞∞∞∞∞∞∞∞∞∞∞∞∞∞∞∞∞∞

This science is very weird. Remember the movie *The Matrix*? Humans lived in a cocoon-type existence with the program of their illusionary reality plugged into their backs and necks by a couple of cables. When the cables were detached, that reality didn't exist anymore. According to Quantum Physics, that is similar to our reality. Unless we pay attention, nothing exists as matter. It goes back to the field and waits there as a potentiality.

Where does that beautiful screensaver go when you activate your computer?

The bottom line for Quantum Physics is there is no bottom line. Matter comes and goes into and out of existence as a result of our attention. Or as a result of being measured in some way by some thing. How in the world does that work? They haven't figured it out yet, but it is a scientific fact, and we make it happen.

∞∞∞∞∞∞∞∞∞∞∞∞∞∞∞∞∞∞∞

It is well known in the field of physics that if a scientist is conducting an experiment with light for example, whatever that scientist is trying to measure is how light will appear. The smallest measurement of light is called a *photon*. It is a particle and it is a wave. Sometimes it will be one or the other. What determines this is what the scientist who is conducting the experiment is looking for. If the scientist is measuring for a particle, then light will be a particle. If the scientist is measuring for a wave, then light will be a wave. Quantum Physics says the person performing the experiment has an effect on the experiment.

In Classical Physics this is heresy. For an experiment to be valid it must be uncontaminated by the person performing the experiment. In Quantum Physics the person performing the experiment is part of the process and has an effect on what will happen. There is no way around this. That puts the human being right smack in the middle of the creation process.

∞∞∞∞∞∞∞∞∞∞∞∞∞∞∞∞∞∞∞

In Classical Physics it was thought that the space between material things was just that—space. There was nothing there. It was empty. Now we know that isn't true. Now we know that so-called empty space is full of energy. In fact, it has been said that there is enough energy in a teaspoon of empty space in front of your face to heat every ocean on the planet to a boil. It is called the Zero Point Field, the Vacuum, the Quantum Soup, Universal Oneness, the Cosmos, the Source, Wu Chi, Mu, the Void . . . God. It is from where everything comes.

When the electrons of atoms come into and out of existence, it is from the Zero Point Field that they come. Every bit of matter in existence has come from the nothingness of the Zero Point Field. I can't show you the formulas, but rest assured that this where everything comes from in our physical plane.

How else can an atom begin? How do things get here? Where did the earth come from? How did your hair grow on your body? Where did that flower come from?

The fact is everything comes from nothing.

Perhaps you answered that God made them. You would be right. But God isn't some old white guy with a beard, unless of course you want him to be.

Einstein's theory of relativity with its famous equation $e = mc^2$ tells us that all matter is made from the same thing. If we break down every bit of matter in the universe, it will result in the same thing—energy.

When energy vibrates, it turns into different things. Some things are hot dogs, some are butterflies, and some are baseball players. According to Quantum Physics, we humans have a lot to do with what a certain portion of energy is going to become in the physical world. It begins when we think.

Quantum Physicists believe the things we see every day, the world we live in, are only there because we all agree they should be. How crazy is that? It is as if all the people on the planet voted for trees to be green. When the blue tree lobby gathers enough energetic power, the trees will be blue. As silly as that may sound, that is a mainstream concept in modern physics.

Some believe there are an infinite number of universes where everything that could possibly happen exists in whatever combination you choose. That is another way of thinking in the Quantum Physics world.

One of the latest theories in Quantum Physics is String Theory. It says there are at least eleven dimensions. String Theory also says that all things are made of the smallest identifiable thing called a *string*, which is energy vibrating at a certain frequency. The vibrational differences determine the physical appearance.

What is entirely true? No one knows, but we can create. The way some things manifest into physical reality is a result of patterns, memories, and forms in the Zero Point Field, some of which are put there by us.

How does a tree know it is supposed to be a tree? How does a leg know it is supposed to be a leg? How do birds know where to go when they migrate? All of that information is imprinted in the field.

∞∞∞∞∞∞∞∞∞∞∞∞∞∞∞∞∞∞∞

Human Creation

As you sow, so shall you reap.
What goes around comes around.
You become what you think about.

How does this happen?
Confused?
You must choose to be.

∞∞∞∞∞∞∞∞∞∞∞∞∞∞∞∞∞∞∞∞

Morphic Resonance

"Thy kingdom come, on earth, as it is in heaven."

The Lord's Prayer

A British biologist named Rupert Sheldrake shook up the biology community in 1982 when he published *A New Science of Life*. His assertions were that instead of all things in biology being only chemical occurrences, there was something else going on. He calls it Morphic Resonance. It is the process of attracting information from the field.

For a long time there have been fields recognized in the world of the sciences. The gravitational field was discovered by Newton in the seventeenth century. The electromagnetic field was discovered by Maxwell in the nineteenth century. Fields are very well accepted in classical science. Morphogenic fields are recognized in biology as the place where a species trying to come into existence gets its information.

∞∞∞∞∞∞∞∞∞∞∞∞∞∞∞∞∞∞∞

In a Japanese experiment with monkeys in the 1950s, when a monkey on an island went to the shore and washed his food, pretty soon all the monkeys of the same type were washing their food as part of their natural makeup. There was no contact between the monkeys on the island and the monkeys on the mainland, but they all started to wash their food. No e-mail was sent to all monkeys saying it was cool to wash your food. How did they know?

When birds that migrate are separated from other birds of their species from birth, they still know when it is time to migrate. How? And how do they know where to go? Morphic Resonance says there is an imprint on the morphogenic field left there by all the other birds throughout time. So when a bird of that type is born, she just picks up her bird form automatically and gets all that information. Its like everything comes standard with this model, no extras are needed. The process is like a radio signal being sent out for help. A new little bird is born and immediately it sends out signals to the universe that say, "I'm a new little bird and I don't know how to do anything and I don't know about anything. HELP!" Before you know it the little bird is getting all the bird info it needs including a detailed map and alarm clock about migration. She gets it all without even having an auto club membership. She gets it by vibrating her DNA.

∞∞∞∞∞∞∞∞∞∞∞∞∞∞∞∞∞∞

Imagine the Zero Point Field as a kind of hard drive. On this drive are stored zillions and zillions of programs. Everything and everyone has millions of programs by which we create our reality. Every part of our body, every part of our humanity, has programs that are used to help us exist and operate. When we are being formed in the womb, our genes send signals to form us in a certain way based on the fact that our genes are human genes and specific from our parents. They send signals to the field that may say, "Okay, we want to create a leg, we need to run a leg program." So the leg program stored in the field is run and tuned and shaped to the type of leg dictated by the gene pool you come from. Genes are like a user interface. They are like the keyboard or perhaps even a mouse that we only have to point.

Things resonate with each other and attract each other until they become physical reality. It is as if there is one big human-being program containing an uncountable number of subprograms for everything from our bodies, to our minds, to our collective behavior, to every situation humans can find themselves in. We draw on the experiences of the entire human population that ever lived and we add to the program to create improvements as we go along our way. Most of what we add is not done consciously, just as what we use is not used consciously. It is from this information placed in the field and withdrawn from the field billions and billions of times that the concept of the earth as we know it is derived. This is what I mean when I say the world is as it is because we all agree. Therein lies the real opportunity for a major paradigm shift in human beings. We are already programmers; we just have to learn how to do it consciously. Computer programs are automated recipes.

∞∞∞∞∞∞∞∞∞∞∞∞∞∞∞∞∞∞∞

It isn't that we have to learn how to do it, we already know how. The process is called habit on an individual level and societal norms on a larger scale. Whatever we do is imprinted into the field. The more it is reinforced, the stronger it becomes. If enough monkeys wash their food, it becomes the norm. If you think a certain way or do certain things, the more you reinforce it, the stronger it becomes. It isn't caused by character deficiencies or strengths, it is science. Of course character deficiencies and strengths dictate what the program will do or form. So it is a good idea to watch how you think and behave. If we all act like morons we will get a moron society. We only have to look at history to know that is a fact.

If you believe we reincarnate, the field is the place you carry your Karma from previous lives. It is the place where the things you do are recorded. What goes around comes around, comes from the field and resonates back at you because things that resonate at the same or harmonic frequencies attract each other.

∞∞∞∞∞∞∞∞∞∞∞∞∞∞∞∞∞∞∞

Smiling for Eden

Perfection, complete harmony, absolute love.
A few of the descriptions of what is striving to come into the physical.

All the things we call evil are small individual ego trips delaying the
process.

Knock it off.
If you are not doing it, stop tolerating it.

Wars, hate, greed are but a few of the despicables created by the minds of
the unknowing.
Let us begin by smiling as we clean up the mess.

∞∞∞∞∞∞∞∞∞∞∞∞∞∞∞∞∞∞∞∞∞

Chaos Mathematics

"Chaos is a friend of mine."

Bob Dylan, Singer

We all have a great appreciation for the steady rhythmic heartbeat inside our chests. We believe a more personal example of machine-like function couldn't be found. Except for one thing, it is not as rhythmic as we think. In fact our hearts beat in a chaotic fashion. The only time it beats with a regular steady frequency is when we are ready to die. The rest of the time our hearts beat with a rhythm that is always changing slightly. Almost, but never quite the same each time it beats. This contributes greatly to the heart's ability to last as long as it does. The whole thing gets exercised this way.

Remember our heart is a big muscle. The various chambers and parts are designed for different functions. If it beats in exactly the same way every single time, the entire organ would not be exercised and would stop functioning. If you sat in a chair perfectly still and lifted a five-pound barbell in one hand up and down and did no other exercise you would have a strong arm, but the rest of your body would be useless.

Our hearts beat in a disorderly fashion. Disorder is good. Now there is a statement not used very much in the world of Classical Physics.

∞∞∞∞∞∞∞∞∞∞∞∞∞∞∞∞∞∞∞∞∞

In the pristine world of Classical Physics there popped up now and then some stuff nobody knew what to do with. Some extra stuff that didn't fit the theory. It was pretty hard to measure what are called *dynamical systems*. There were too many variables. So they just called the extra stuff "noise" and forgot about it.

Scientists began to understand that the universe didn't operate in the orderly fashion predicted by classical science. They began to see that most things were nonlinear. A new field was created in mathematics to deal with the nonlinearity or the dynamical. Somehow it got the name

Chaos Theory of Mathematics. I don't know why it is called Chaos when it is actually just the opposite. Chaos Math helped to get rid of the chaos and make prediction of behavior in dynamical or constantly moving systems possible.

In the 1970s a mathematician named Benoit Mandelbratt, who worked for IBM, was able to use the computer to create a visual image of these chaotic formations. He created something called the Mandelbratt Sets; these are the visual interpretations of the constant feedback created by a formula being fed back upon itself. It creates a flowing, beautiful visual effect of change. He showed the dance of life. This could not been seen prior to the advances made with computer technology.

Another scientist studying meteorology in the 1960s named Edward Lorenz came up with the so-called *butterfly effect*. The butterfly effect is the idea that if a butterfly flapped its wings in Brazil, a tornado may occur sometime later in Texas. It is the quintessential model for cause and effect. The butterfly pushes a little air that joins with some more air moving for another reason. The combined air in turn joins with some more moving air; before you know it you have a tornado.

Mandelbratt also worked with something called *fractal geometry*. It is very difficult for a non-mathematician to explain and understand, but the gist is that an infinite amount of information can be put into a limited space.

Mandelbratt said, if you were to measure the coastline of somewhere using a yardstick you are going to get a certain measurement, obviously. If you then measure it again using a foot-long ruler you will get a different number that is larger. The yardstick couldn't fit into some of the nooks and crannies that the ruler could. If you then continue to measure using progressively smaller tools, the coastline will get progressively longer. This apparently can go on forever, which theoretically makes the coastline of infinite length. This says an infinite amount of information can be put into a finite space.

∞∞∞∞∞∞∞∞∞∞∞∞∞∞∞∞∞∞

The real cool thing about fractal geometry is that it measures things in different dimensions. For instance, if you watch a ball coming toward you in the air, when it is far away it appears to be a two-dimensional object. As it gets closer to you, at some point it changes to a three-dimensional object. What is it at the exact moment the ball shifts between the second dimension and the third dimension? Mandelbratt called that shift a *fractal*—a change in phase space.

Think of a tree. A tree begins to grow with the trunk beginning to grow straight up. At some point a branch decides to grow out of the trunk in a different direction. The branch then decides to split off smaller branches each time in a different direction. Each time this occurs, a fractal or change in phase space makes it happen until the tree is fully grown into the particular shape the tree genes tell it to be. The process of the splitting and changing is fractal geometry, an integral part of Chaos Mathematics. The exact shape and the number of branches are determined in part by the need of the particular tree to maximize its surface to get sunlight and water.

Your lungs too are chaotic in their design. The bronchial tubes create fractal after fractal until the smallest bronchia is created. It is all folded up inside your chest cavity. It is said that the total area of your lungs, if laid out flat, would fill a tennis court. Chaos mathematics is at play to create order from what appears to be a random development so maximum efficiency can be attained.

∞∞∞∞∞∞∞∞∞∞∞∞∞∞∞∞∞∞

It used to be thought that certain things were not measurable. The "noise" mentioned before. How do you measure and predict which way water will go and how much spray will occur in a shallow, swiftly running stream? How about when you put milk in your coffee and just watch it gently swirl. Do you think you can measure that and predict how the swirls will form? You can't exactly, but you can get very close. The answer is Chaos Mathematics.

The weather is probably the best commonly known example of the difficulties found in measuring. How many variables do you suppose are present when meteorologists attempt to forecast the weather, say a month from now? The number must be in the hundreds of millions, perhaps billions. Which is why today, even with the best technology and massive computing power, it is still impossible to get it exactly correct. We can predict tomorrow's weather in a certain spot pretty accurately. We can get close a couple days out. But we cannot, even for the next few hours, be absolutely perfect in our predictions of what the weather will do. It is constantly moving and constantly changing. It develops in patterns, not absolutes. The weather is a dynamical system. Dynamical systems were ignored for hundreds of years because nobody could get close to figuring them out. We made great strides with the clear and orderly measurements we were able to make over the centuries; the problem is most of the world, and indeed the universe, is like the weather—chaotic. There are countless variables.

∞∞∞∞∞∞∞∞∞∞∞∞∞∞∞∞∞∞∞

There are things called *Attractors* that enable the scientist to understand how order comes from chaos. Imagine a ball spinning in a cone. As it travels around and around, it travels downward toward the middle of the cone. Gravity is drawing it down, but there is a point that is drawing the ball to it. That point is an Attractor. When an Attractor draws things to it, the things it draws come together at that point. The Super Bowl is an Attractor. How many millions are drawn to their TV sets each year. The smile of a baby attracts smiles from every normal person who sees it. There are millions of Attractors in operation constantly all around us. Big and small. Insignificant and monumental.

Let's go back to the destructive butterfly. When those wings flap, a vortex of air is created that is moving in a certain direction. As it moves air, it will either get stronger or die down. It will get stronger as it pulls in more air. It will then attract more air, which will in turn make it stronger yet. Before you know it, a full-blown tornado is sweeping across the land sucking everything in its path into a very strong vortex. All attracted by a killer butterfly. Of course you can't pin it all on the butterfly. If you could it would fit neatly into a Classical Physics model.

The reason Chaos is so difficult to predict is that there are numerous variables that make the calculation of real precision almost impossible.

A tornado is the result of just the right combination of uncountable variables all coming together at precisely the right time. The butterfly may be one, but not the only one, so don't go out and hunt down all the butterflies in your neighborhood just yet.

∞∞∞∞∞∞∞∞∞∞∞∞∞∞∞∞∞∞

As I was watching the events of 9/11 on my TV unfolding a few miles from my home, I remember thinking this is a Strange Attractor for hate. Don't ask me why, but Attractors involving human beings are called *Strange Attractors*. Scientists seem to have a warped sense of humor. Feelings and emotions are things also; this does not only apply to material objects. If one person in a family is in a bad mood, unless we are careful, soon everyone will be in the same bad mood. Those feelings and emotions associated with the bad mood are Attractors.

Human behavior can be measured by Chaos Mathematics. Ever since we were attacked on 9/11, there hasn't been much good will and love in the world. We have had death and destruction all around the planet. Most of it in the name of so-called good. Violence brings violence, and love brings love. This can now be measured scientifically.

Chaos enables us to measure the dance that is life. We are not mechanistic beings, and our world is not a machine. The so-called *noise*, which has been ignored in our scientific world, is in fact the beautiful underlying order of the universe that will take humanity another step toward understanding the incredible beauty that is implicit in our reality.

This wasn't figured out until the 1970s because the computer wasn't around. To do the calculation necessary to show this theory takes immense amounts of computing power. It can't be done by hand.

∞∞∞∞∞∞∞∞∞∞∞∞∞∞∞∞∞∞

Chaos Mathematics and the concept of Attractors changed the way we view cause and effect. Instead of our becoming and obtaining what we get in life as a result of a series of events that culminate in our present reality, Chaos and the concept of Attractors say we are pulled into our current reality by what is attracting us into the future. As an example, if you decide you want to be a singer, and you become successful, what is the reason? Most would say it was as a result of hard work and study. Unending hours of practice and dedication gets you to the end result. If you focus on the work necessary with diligence you will succeed.

That is all true. It is the Newtonian model and it is a fact. But what started the ball rolling? It was the Attractor, "I want to be a singer."

The Attractor and the focus on the Attractor is what brought about the action needed to accomplish the goal. If the thought process didn't stay on the end goal in a dedicated, focused way, nothing would have happened. So what was the cause and what was the effect? Many say you need not do anything but remain focused on the outcome with a passion and a belief it already exists, and the things you need to do to make it happen will come to you automatically. This is Chaos Mathematics at work.

∞∞∞∞∞∞∞∞∞∞∞∞∞∞∞∞∞∞∞

Effect as Cause

Our minds move energy.
Energy knows no time.

Our thoughts are things, just like our socks.
Create a thought, put it in the future.

When I see myself writing a book,
I send it a lot of energy.

Soon it will be physical.
It was real from the moment it was thought.

If you doubt this works,
It won't.

You still have to do the writing,
But it is easier if you start here.

∞∞∞∞∞∞∞∞∞∞∞∞∞∞∞∞∞∞∞∞

The Technology

The Human Body

"I picture John physically as someone youthful who made a lot, but I feel him more as energy, more metaphysically."

George Harrison, Beatle

The human body is the most fantastic piece of technology ever created. It must be made stronger than other animals, because no animal alive is ever seen abusing their bodies the way we humans do. I've never owned a dog that smoked cigarettes or a cat that ate too many donuts. Human beings have invented thousands of ways to bring physical harm to themselves, but the body still stays strong and resists damage with an unbelievable strength. Try getting a car to last 80 or 90 years while putting bad fuel into it and hardly ever changing the oil. That is the equivalent of what most of us do to our bodies. We are blessed. Our bodies are strong. Even when we abuse them, they still function.

The practice of Western medicine has made enormous strides in the past 100 years. Many of the diseases that had wiped out entire populations have been controlled or eradicated completely. The advances in the pharmaceutical industry just since the 1950s have been phenomenal. Today, we have drugs that are targeted with pinpoint accuracy toward the ailment they are produced to treat. Technologies in use for disease detection have also taken amazing leaps over what was available just a short time ago. Doctors have at their disposal the means of looking at the entire human body and are able to make diagnoses today that people not very long ago would have thought supernatural.

Our technological advances in medicine, as good as they are, may be the exact opposite of what we really need. We may be addicting ourselves to the use of outside substances instead of learning to allow our bodies to heal themselves.

I am not advocating the cessation of any treatment the medical community may have prescribed for you, but a little thought should go into what we do. We can develop a society of people who are in charge of their own health. Our bodies are remarkable, if we develop their functionality we can learn to heal ourselves at the minimum.

∞∞∞∞∞∞∞∞∞∞∞∞∞∞∞∞∞∞∞∞∞

In treating the human body, Western medicine recognizes the circulatory system, the respiratory system, the nervous system, the digestive system, and other systems they can see. Westerners are just now beginning to understand there is an energy system as well in the human body. We can't see it yet, but it is there.

Energy flows from the field into our bodies. It is what keeps us alive just as much as the air we breathe. The ancient Asians discovered a system of energy meridians that connect our various organs directly to the energy of the cosmos. Along these meridians are over 300 little vortices or little whirlpool-like spots where energy comes into and out of our bodies. It is the manipulation of these spots, either by pressure in the practice of acupressure or with needles in the case of acupuncture, which is at the core of Eastern medicine. Thousands of years ago they knew if your meridians were not open and your energy was not flowing properly, then your health would deteriorate. If your energy meridians are open however, your physical health will improve greatly and your organs will function as they should. They will be getting the proper amount of energy necessary for healthy function. The practice of Chiropractic Medicine is based on a similar premise. If your spine is not aligned properly, then the energy flowing through your body will be pinched off and disease will result. Chiropractors have been telling us that for many years.

We know what happens when the circulatory system is blocked. If we don't get the proper amount of blood to a vital organ or some other part of our body, that part dies. In the case of a vital organ, it usually takes the whole body with it. Blocked energy meridians are the same. We just can't see them when we cut open the body.

Only recently have Western insurance companies begun to appreciate the value of the Eastern practices of acupuncture and acupressure.

The energy system may, in fact, be the most important system in the entire body. This may be so not only from a physical health point of view, but also from the point of view of the future of human development.

∞∞∞∞∞∞∞∞∞∞∞∞∞∞∞∞∞∞∞∞

Another, perhaps more important feature of the energy system of the body, besides helping to keep us physically healthy, is what else happens to our bodies when our energy is free flowing.

Remember information also comes from the field. When your body is open and your energy is flowing unimpeded, not only do you get healthier, but you also get better information from the field into your brain. Synchronicities increase, intuition grows, and sometimes you just know things without any explanation. You can believe this comes directly from God, or you may look at it as a scientific equation. Or, you may consider it a scientific equation created by God. Have it any way you like, it is your view of the world that is being created. It is your recipe.

Remember the pictures you saw of saints with halos? A halo is an energy emanation. Remember the pictures of Christ and the saints with their arms outstretched and rays of light shining out of their palms? That is energy from the cosmos shining through their bodies. Everyone's body is capable of this. We need not be a saint. Or, perhaps the energy helps us become one. Some call it Holy Spirit.

It really doesn't have all that much to do with what kind of religious book you read or what kind of clothes you wear; it has to do with the science of the human body. It is actually a matter of getting the technological genius of the human body tuned in to the universe the way it was intended. This could begin to happen with one thought.

Our bodies are highly sophisticated pieces of technology. They are far more important things than most of us use them for. They really are our spirit's means of remembering why we are here, and the technology for connecting ourselves back to where we came from.

Small children are usually more sensitive to who we really are as humans than most adults. When we are young, our ego hasn't been hardened to the so-called realities of our earthly existence and we still have a glimpse of our true self. As we age, we tend to lose that innocence and become so-called *normal* human beings.

If you master the tools, practicing the best recipe for you, the body will flow with the energy of a newly arrived spirit.

∞∞∞∞∞∞∞∞∞∞∞∞∞∞∞∞∞∞∞∞

The human body is a miraculous creation. With the spirit of the divine flowing into our bodies, there is nothing we cannot do. So what does this all mean? If we get our energy meridians open will we be like saints with rays flowing from our hands and halos around our heads? Will we be able to perform miracles? Some may, most will not. But you certainly will be healthier. And if society were to evolve where the concepts put forth in the three sciences were part of the culture, we would have a whole lot more "saints" in our midst. Eventually humanity would advance to the next level.

Three sciences and one piece of technology. We don't even have to understand the sciences. We simply have to know how to use the technology.

There are people right now who can do amazing things with energy and the control of energy. Actually, control is probably not the right word; *allowing* is probably closer to what we need to do to properly use the energy that comes from God.

There are various practices to help you open the energy meridians in you body. Most cultures have some type of energy training. All take full advantage of the specific value and contribution of each tool.

∞∞∞∞∞∞∞∞∞∞∞∞∞∞∞∞∞∞∞∞

Technology 101

The heart is the seat of the soul.
It is through the heart we realize our humanity.

The brain is the connector.
It is with the brain our spirit stays connected to the divine.

The technology that is the human body can be tuned like a concert piano.
And played like a virtuoso.

The whole thing runs on pure energy. And it's free.

∞∞∞∞∞∞∞∞∞∞∞∞∞∞∞∞∞∞

The Tools

"Man is a tool-using animal."

Thomas Carlyle, Essayist

We have talked about the sciences that make things happen and we have talked about our greatest technology—the human body—but how do we get these things to work for us as individuals? We must use the tools that come with the technology, the rest of the ingredients.

What follows is a brief description of each of the tools available to the human being. Remember, this is a guide; it will not show you how to use the tools described here. The specific use of these tools is determined by the particular recipe you choose. It would not make sense for me to expound on each of these. There are already tons of books written on each. For instance, a quick search of the Internet for the word *thought* brings dozens and dozens of books written about the various aspects and views on the idea of thought.

Any time you have ever wanted something in your life, these are the tools you used to bring it about. These are the tools you use to perpetuate your existence on earth. Mastery of these tools is taught by all the great disciplines.

Thoughts

"All that we are is the result of what we think. The mind is everything. What we think we become."

Buddha

I'm not sure anyone has clearly figured out what thought is. Our brains have a process where brain cells called *neurons* fire off electrical energy and create little connections called *synapses*, which many scientists have concluded have much to do with the thought process. Thought is the product of our minds, but we are not even sure where our mind is located. We used to think it was located entirely in the brain, but that has changed over the years. Now the acceptable theory is that our mind is not only made up of our brain, but of our entire body and by areas outside our physical body.

Many cultures believe we have more than one body. Some think our minds are also parts of these other non-visible bodies. The answer to these questions will come undeniably sometime down the road. For this effort, it isn't necessary to define the location of the mind; it is simply necessary to understand that thoughts are things. Where exactly they are created is not as important as how we deal with our thoughts.

Remember, Einstein's discovery $e = mc^2$ proved that everything is energy. So thoughts are energy. What makes things different is the vibrational frequency of energy. One thing may vibrate at frequency A and become an atom of copper. Another thing may vibrate at frequency B and become an atom of gold. Another could vibrate at frequency C and become the idea that brings about world peace or the cure for cancer.

Our thoughts, which are things, vibrate at certain frequencies. As we send our thoughts out into the universe they attract things that vibrate at the same or a harmonic frequency. We must be sure they are vibrating as we desire. We want our thoughts to resonate with what we are looking for.

This isn't magnetism where opposites attract; this is something different where like attracts like. It is like a tuning fork, which when struck will cause another nearby fork of the same frequency to vibrate. This is reaping what you sow.

Our thoughts are one of the tools.

∞∞∞∞∞∞∞∞∞∞∞∞∞∞∞∞∞∞∞

Moods

Moods are thoughts magnified by emotion.
They are easy to construct and quite contagious.
They can be grown or caused to disappear.
We can learn to change them at will.

If our thoughts are good and we add the correct dose of joy we can bring
about a pleasant mood.

If our thoughts are bad or frightening they lead us to an
emotion of the same.
Then we are in a nasty place.

The art is to make sure the thoughts we have control the emotions.
We let thought become an Attractor when emotion is added.

It is up to us to choose.
We simply have to watch and think about it.

∞∞∞∞∞∞∞∞∞∞∞∞∞∞∞∞∞∞∞∞

Emotions

"I do not literally paint that table, but the emotion it produces upon me."

Henri Matisse, Painter

Feel the emotion of Joy. Notice I didn't say think the emotion of Joy. Emotions are not thoughts. They are not formed in the mind. They come with your body. Emotions are actually physical reactions to various peptides and amino acids contained in our body. This was proven by microbiologist Dr. Candice Pert. In her book *Molecules of Emotion*, she shares the results of her research, which shows that emotions are created by and stored in our bodies. Most people in the world do not know this. Most are like me who thought emotions were the product of our minds. They may be triggered by our minds, but they are not created there. Our minds can only produce thought. Plain old unemotional thought.

There are many reports of patients having very emotional responses to certain procedures being performed on various parts of the body. There are reports of people getting angry or laughing uncontrollably for no apparent reason while having a chiropractic manipulation or while undergoing a Rolfing procedure or deep tissue massage. When the place where a particular emotion is stored is agitated, the emotion will appear.

So let us ponder the emotion of joy. If you think, "I am joyous," are you? Perhaps eventually, but not immediately. The thought "I am joyous" must first be processed. When first said, it has the same emotional power as saying anything else—none. It is when the thought triggers the emotion of joy, which in turn triggers the feeling of joy, that you become joyous.

Maybe you won't become joyous simply by making the statement. Most likely you will sit there and feel nothing. This is where the art of acting comes into play. A good actor has command of her emotions. When the thought comes into her mind "I am joyous," she can immediately remember the feeling of joy, access the emotion of joy, and be joyous.

Most of the rest of us need a joyous experience or event to feel the emotion of joy. The actor is well trained at faking it until the stored emotion is triggered. They create Attractors.

Control your emotions! We have all heard the phrase. It means what I just said the actor does. Conscious thought taking charge of an attribute of the body—the emotions. The actor brings them forth consciously. That is why they call it *emoting*. Most of us do the opposite. We use our minds to stifle our emotions.

I once worked with a man who I thought was the most controlled person I had ever met. This guy never showed any sign of emotion. He was the same all of the time. When things were going bad you couldn't tell by looking at him. You could also not tell when things were going great. He was in control of his emotions as far as suppressing them better than anyone I knew. We worked in a field where a lot of negotiating took place, so a poker face was an extreme advantage. He was a great negotiator. Nobody could read him. As fate would have it, he developed Parkinson's disease. Parkinson's is a disease where at a certain point the emotions are unleashed without any conscious trigger. One moment the person will be fine and appear perfectly normal, the next he may be crying like a baby.

Parkinson's is a disease that proves to me that the emotions are stored in the body. I thought it ironic that the man I knew as the most controlled would be afflicted with a disease that causes complete loss of control. I once asked my friend, before he was ill, how he came to be able to control his emotions in such a stoic fashion. He told me he got that way after attending U.S. Marine Corps Boot Camp.

There are numerous ways to learn things. The best usually involves a physical experience.

Emotions are physical. They are stored chemical recipes that feed our feelings. If we allow.

∞∞∞∞∞∞∞∞∞∞∞∞∞∞∞∞∞∞∞∞∞

Emotions

I sent a message to heaven.
I would like to write about emotions.

Calm down I was told.
You are getting impatient.

Do not worry about the outcome, simply write.
And you will be happy with the result.
I didn't get angry, I listened.

Now I am grateful.

∞∞∞∞∞∞∞∞∞∞∞∞∞∞∞∞∞∞∞

Feelings

"The biggest disease this day and age is that of people feeling unloved."

Diana, British Princess

How do you feel? You hurt my feelings. I'm not sure how I feel about it. I've got to get a feel for it. Thank you for your heartfelt greeting. See how this feels.

All of these are statements regarding feelings, but did you ever really think about feelings. There are two kinds of feelings; physical, as in "I felt pain in my leg," and emotional, as in "How do these words make you feel?" Most of us never really analyze and feel our feelings, we usually just react to them. We react to feelings with emotion, and vice versa.

Let's try something. Just for a minute. I would like you to take off your wristwatch and put in front of you or place a clock in front of you. I assume you are sitting down. That is how we usually read. We are going to feel our bodies.

What I would like you to do is to sit quietly and just feel your body. When you are finished reading these instructions, I want you to look at the watch and note the second hand. Watch it move. Now close your eyes and just feel your body for one minute. Don't think. Just feel. If you feel a physical sensation in your leg or your arm or your stomach or some other part of your body, don't give it a name, which would be thinking. Just feel it. Stay with it without thinking about it. Keep your attention on the feeling for a complete minute without judging it, naming it, or thinking about it in any way. Just feel it. If it goes away, find another and move your attention there. When you think a whole minute has passed of pure uninterrupted feeling, open your eyes and look at the watch. Okay, stop reading and begin.

Welcome back. How much time has passed? Most likely you didn't make the whole minute of pure feeling. It is not how we have conditioned ourselves. We haven't developed the skill to just feel. We are usually too busy thinking.

How about the other kind of feeling? The emotional kind. That seems to be even more difficult to just feel. At least with the physical we have the assistance of a location in space to assist us. Our leg is a place. We can put our attention there. When we have an emotional feeling it is not possible to pinpoint a place where our attention should be. Our emotions may be stored in our physical bodies, but the feelings that accompany them are somewhere else. What does it feel like to be angry? I don't mean what are the consequences of being angry, like the physical reactions of raised blood pressure and any other accompanying response. I mean the actual feeling itself. I am not sure the actual feeling can be defined in words. I think it can only be felt. But it can be remembered. It can be remembered and stored for future reference. Feelings are important tools in the process of making things happen. The earth has been shaped by feelings.

One of the most profound examples of the earth being shaped by feelings has to be what President of the United States Harry Truman felt in August of 1945. He was faced with a decision of whether or not to authorize the use of the first nuclear weapon in the history of the planet. Don't think about this now with the information you have in your brain regarding nuclear weapons. That all came about after Truman made the decision. Perhaps if he knew what you know, he would have made a different decision. He said afterward he wouldn't, but who knows.

Let us go back to what he must have been feeling. He was the Commander-in-Chief during a war encompassing the entire world. Japan was all but defeated. Perhaps the United States could have isolated them and ended it differently. That is not relevant for this exercise. Whatever the options he was presented, he had to have given the matter great thought. How many American lives would be lost in the invasion of Japan? Estimates said hundreds of thousands could possibly die. How many civilians would die? What would be the effect on the future of mankind? Question after question must have gone through his mind. All thoughts.

He obviously encountered a lot of emotional experience while contemplating this decision. Anger that he was in the position, sadness over the loss of lives that would ensue either way, perhaps joy over having a solution to end a bitter conflict that had already killed so many.

The planet-changing decision, however, was made based on what Harry Truman felt. All the information he received, all the emotion he experienced, only contributed to creating a feeling inside him of what was the right thing to do. It was based on that feeling that the action took place. Think about that. The entire history of the planet was changed based on one feeling by one man.

This may seem like an oversimplification, but it isn't. If you say there were many factors that need to be considered, you would be right. If you said a decision of this nature was too complex to be brought down to the feeling of one man, you would be wrong. The entire Cold War with its nuclear threat, the ominous cloud of nuclear destruction hanging over the head of humanity was based on one feeling. Someone else surely would have made the decision later; humanity had the bomb and it was almost inevitable that it would be used. All that is true, but the actual decision was based on what Truman felt the day he gave the okay. Perhaps the most profound effect of an individual feeling in the history of the planet. Feelings shape the world in which we live. Thankfully, we are not in the situation President Truman was in then, but every time we act on a feeling, we are shaping the world in some way. Every single time.

Try this. Read this section again. Only this time as you read, take your time to think about every sentence. Feel the impact the knowledge is having. Not just on your brain, but on your whole body. Take your time and feel what you read.

You will find that our feelings are closely tied to our emotions. They seem to be interrelated. An emotion will trigger a feeling, and a feeling may trigger an emotion. Many think they are the same things. They are not.

Perhaps one of the best descriptions I have ever heard of feeling is by Greg Braden, author of the *Isaiah Effect* and other great books and audio programs. He calls feeling the "language" between thought and emotion. I attended one of Greg's seminars and it was a real treat. Greg presents a seminar where the participants experience a miracle and understand how natural it is for human beings to do so. He helps you feel it.

∞∞∞∞∞∞∞∞∞∞∞∞∞∞∞∞∞

Feelings

Feelings can be studied.
They can be analyzed.

Feelings can be written about.
They can't be known until they are felt.

∞∞∞∞∞∞∞∞∞∞∞∞∞∞∞∞∞∞∞∞∞

Beliefs

"It is not disbelief that is dangerous to our society, it is belief."

George Bernard Shaw, Playwright

What you believe shapes your world and everyone who comes into contact with you. Beliefs are commonly thought of in religious terms, but our beliefs encompass more than just the manner in which we do or do not choose to worship God.

You may believe that a certain thing is the way it is because someone in your life kept providing you with information about that thing on a constant basis until you absolutely knew in your heart it was the truth. One of the great examples frequently used to illustrate this is Roger Bannister and the four-minute mile.

Prior to Bannister breaking the record and becoming the first human known to run a mile in under four minutes, the world believed it was not humanly possible to run that fast. It was a recognized "fact" accepted by most people.

It wasn't until May 6, 1954, when the British medical student ran the mile in 3 minutes 59.4 seconds, that the beliefs of the entire human race shifted and "impossibility" became reality. The month after Bannister changed world thinking, an Australian runner named John Landy broke Bannister's record. Once the barrier was broken, the feat was accomplished many times over in a relatively short period of time. The Roger Bannister story is the perfect example of how human beings are held back by limiting beliefs.

Religious beliefs are some of the most powerful. This is understandable since the concept of religion is one of indoctrinating people with information that for the most part cannot be proven and must be taken on faith and simply believed. Because of this, religions have developed methods of continuously involving the faithful in a never-ending recitation of the dogma to be believed. After a time people take these beliefs to be fact. Much of the death and destruction in the history of the planet came about as a result of people acting on their religious beliefs. It is still happening in this modern time. I find it ironic that people slaughter others in the name of God, who is supposed to be peaceful and loving.

The power of belief is a very powerful dynamic force in human behavior. It is also a dynamic force in how we view the physical world. Science tells us our physical reality is an illusion and the existence of the universe as we view it is really dependent on our belief that it is the way we believe it to be. I'm not sure people are ready for the truth in terms of exactly what our physical reality looks like. Who knows, someday we may all be looking at each other and seeing a vibrating cloud of energy instead of the human form we now see.

Our beliefs, both in terms of what we believe or disbelieve, play a major part in shaping our reality.

∞∞∞∞∞∞∞∞∞∞∞∞∞∞∞∞∞∞∞

Believe

He said we could all do it.
The same as Him.

According to Matt some were shown.
We must have faith.
Didn't anybody pass it on?

∞∞∞∞∞∞∞∞∞∞∞∞∞∞∞∞∞∞∞

Allowing

Allowing is relaxing and letting flow be your substance.

I was taught in the martial arts to relax my shoulders and just let my hands go when throwing punches. I thought I knew what it meant until I watched Carl Lewis, the great track star, run a 100-meter race. I don't remember the race—only that it was at the height of Lewis' competitiveness. He won the race handily and was being interviewed afterward when he taught me one of the greatest lessons of my life.

The reporter asked Mr. Lewis what his strategy was for running the race. I thought to myself, are you nuts? Its a hundred meters! What kind of strategy can you have besides get out of the blocks clean and run as fast as you can?

What Carl Lewis said, and what he did when he ran, was incredible. He said, for the first 60 meters he concentrates on getting his body to run as fast as it can possibly go. Then he relaxes and allows it to take him to the finish line. The instant replay showed exactly what he described. At the 60 meter mark Lewis seemed to shift a gear and accelerated down the track. It was as if a field of energy was taking him along. He quickly outdistanced his competition and left them in the dust.

Allowing is trusting. When we allow something into our lives, we trust it will be in our best interest. Sometimes it isn't. Allowing has nothing to do with being right or wrong, it has to do with relaxing. When we trust we can relax. Carl Lewis trusted his body's connection to the energy source. He knew his technology was in tune. He was prepared to pump it up, relax, and trust.

Plenty of people can use the other tools, but many forget to allow. What they think about and desire never gets allowed into their lives. After all that other work, they forgot to teach themselves how to allow their wishes to come into their lives.

Most people allow things into their lives without really understanding just what they are doing. To paraphrase Abe Lincoln, you get to pick how happy you will be. You also get to pick how sad. You pick how rich, how poor, how healthy, how frail. You get to pick it all. Allowing is a tool that is very much misused or forgotten.

∞∞∞∞∞∞∞∞∞∞∞∞∞∞∞∞∞∞

Allowing

I inhale,
I exhale with a sigh.

I hold up my arm,
I let it fall abruptly.

I hold up my legs, my chest, and my head all in their turn,
I let them all fall.

I focus on the feeling of the letting go and the release.
I remember the feeling.

I recall the feeling at will.
This is a way I train to allow things to come into my life.

∞∞∞∞∞∞∞∞∞∞∞∞∞∞∞∞∞∞

Intentions

"The evil that is in the world almost always comes of ignorance, and good intentions may do as much harm as malevolence if they lack understanding."

Albert Camus, Nobelist

I once met a man who was trained by the Maori of New Zealand to be a healer. He was like a witch doctor or a shaman. He learned their ancient secrets for healing. He was also an MD trained in Western medicine, but in his Maori practice he used intention. His technique was to lay his hands on the patient and intend for that person to be healed. I asked him what he thought about as he did this and he told me it didn't make any difference what he thought about as long as his intention was for a healing to occur. He was apparently very successful in helping the people of Chernobyl after the nuclear disaster that occurred there in the 1980s. Other energy healers I have spoken with told me similar things. It is what you intend to happen that will happen when you are using energy to help someone heal.

Intentions are desires. If you want something to happen in a certain way, what you desire as the outcome is your intention. Intentions become Attractors. Remember the Attractor "I want to be a singer"? If you concentrate on a desire hard enough, it will cause you to be presented with certain actions necessary to bring about the desired effect. "I want to be a singer" is an intention. If it is thought about consistently, with the right amount of emotion, it will be an Attractor. It will gain strength, bring suggested actions to your consciousness and, if you allow, it will come about.

Intentions are very powerful tools. Perhaps the most powerful to come with our human form. We must be very careful what we intend. We should be very honest with ourselves in analyzing our actions for an accurate realization of what we intend. Many times people will have a proverbial "hidden agenda." They take certain actions, which on the surface appear intended for one thing, but in reality an entirely different intention is behind the action. Realize also that sometimes you may have a hidden agenda intention that is hidden from yourself. The subconscious mind is very large, and if programmed in a certain manner, can cause you to take actions or express beliefs that you may never have consciously thought through. Be aware of your intentions.

It is also very important to think out what will happen if you take action to bring about your intentions. Human beings do not live in a vacuum. We are all connected and what we do is connected. We may not get quite what we want if we are not careful. We must be alert for unintended consequences.

In the diplomatic arena they call this *blowback*—getting something through your actions that you didn't intend. The most famous example of this is Afghanistan and Al Qaeda. In 1979, the Soviet Union invaded Afghanistan. Since the Soviets were the ideological enemy of the United States, it made sense to the Central Intelligence Agency (CIA) for the Americans to assist the people resisting the Soviet invasion. The American CIA and the Saudi Kingdom provided funds for the resistance fighters. The Soviets were defeated. Many claim it was a major factor in the fall of the Soviet Union. Perhaps it was, but it also had unintended consequences.

The people the CIA was funding in Afghanistan eventually became Al Qaeda. Our intentions in 1979 may have been good from an American CIA point of view. The blowback clearly was not.

Intentions should be clearly thought out.

∞∞∞∞∞∞∞∞∞∞∞∞∞∞∞∞∞∞∞∞

Small Change

Every time I change a few cells, there is a new I.
Every time I help one person become more human, there is a new planet.

You need not be caring and loving to do this.
There is science at work here.

Caring and loving do, however, speed up the process
and make us feel a lot better.

Cells are easy to change.
Intention is the tool.

∞∞∞∞∞∞∞∞∞∞∞∞∞∞∞∞∞∞∞∞

Energy

"Love is energy of life."

Robert Browning, Poet

I spoke before about energy, but there cannot be enough said about this tool. It is the most important thing you could possibly think of. It *is* all things. It is what everything is made of. Chi, Ki, Holy Spirit, whatever you choose to call it, energy is the composition of and the source of all things. The frequency at which it vibrates determines what it will be. Those little strings of quantum theory vibrate at rates which in many cases are determined by you. Energy is everything. When we learn to dance with it we will be like the Gods. This is what Jesus Christ meant when he said we could do the things he did.

Energy is everything. There is nothing else.

∞∞∞∞∞∞∞∞∞∞∞∞∞∞∞∞∞∞

Vibration

The warrior's spirit, the artist's,
The spirit of the good and the bad.
They are all the same.
Except for their vibrational frequency.

You and I are as the Gods,
We simply have to realize it and let ourselves be.
Be still and silent and you will feel yourself,
Be yet more still and silent and you will know everyone.

When you know everyone,
You know the unity there is.
When you live the unity there is,
You would never hurt another.

Humans merely need to develop the skill of changing vibration.
Then all will be now.
The now is eternal.
Hurry Science. Relax people.

∞∞∞∞∞∞∞∞∞∞∞∞∞∞∞∞∞

Other Things

These few things that follow are not tools, as those described previously, but some things we must be aware of and do if the ingredients are to work at their utmost efficiency.

Ego

"God equals man minus ego."

Sri Sathya Sai Baba, Spiritual Leader

Our ego keeps us from insanity. It protects our spirit when we become physical beings. Without the ego it would probably be too difficult to handle the experience of humanity. It is kind of like an interim protection created to ease us into an understanding of who we really are. Unfortunately, the ego tends to take over and likes us to believe it is our true self. It is not. Our true self is a spirit that is part of the oneness that is all things. That may sound like a lot of hooey to some, but it is the truth. Putting it into words will not convince you, nor can it. Experiencing that reality is the only way to know the ego is not who we are.

Many teachings tell us of the need to get past the ego and understand our true reality. Many people interpret this as a condemnation of the ego. It shouldn't be condemned. It is not a bad thing. It shouldn't be destroyed. If it were, you would probably be transformed into some type of socially unfit state resembling sainthood. Most likely you would then be put into a mental institution. Perhaps someday we humans may inhabit the earth without the ego, until then we must try to understand it for what it really is and smile at its antics. Just don't let it run the show. Sainthood will be socially acceptable when it is the majority status, kind of like green trees.

It is very interesting how brilliant the ego can be. For instance, you may be reading this and fully grasp the concepts put forth. Perhaps you even think I am being a little too shallow in my explanations of the ego. You get it. You are very sophisticated. Aren't you proud of yourself?

Is it your spirit which is proud? No, your spirit is detached and just watching how your ego is taking you off track by patting you on the back for understanding that the ego will fool you with self-praise for understanding that you should not let the ego run your life. That is brilliant manipulation.

The purpose of this section is to remind you that the ingredients of making things happen will work best when they are used by your true self. They can be used by the ego; we see the results. Sometimes good, sometime horrific. If they are used by the spirit, we can get heaven on earth. Study the ego, don't let it rule.

∞∞∞∞∞∞∞∞∞∞∞∞∞∞∞∞∞∞

Humble Gods

Were you proud of yourself when you discovered
the ego needed to be transcended?

Did you feel smarter than the person beside you
when you found out we were all one?

It is hard for Gods to be humble.
But you will never be until you are.

∞∞∞∞∞∞∞∞∞∞∞∞∞∞∞∞∞∞∞

Practice

*"An ounce of practice is worth more than
tons of preaching."*

Mahatma Gandhi, Revolutionary

Now that you have the ingredients for how things happen, you must apply them to whatever recipe you choose to make things happen in your life. Perhaps you will use a religious practice where prayer and devotion to God are the means chosen to bring joy to your life. Some may approach these ingredients from a purely scientific angle, analyzing each ingredient and carefully understanding how it is affecting the overall outcome.

There will also be degrees of participation, which will vary across a wide spectrum. Some, perhaps most, may immediately go for the gold and get started on bringing riches to their lives. There are many recipes for attracting wealth. Be careful; if you get stuck in that area you may get very rich, but you may not reach sainthood. You may just create another greedy pig. There is nothing wrong with wealth. There is enough abundance for everyone to have a good life. Just be careful not to get stuck there. The concept of needing to compete for material wealth is a fallacy. It is like saying we should have to compete for sunshine.

Whatever recipe you choose to consciously implement these ingredients, just thinking about them will not suffice. You will be changed simply because you know of these ingredients, but you will not come close to your full potential unless you put into practice whatever recipe you choose.

If you choose prayer, pray a lot. If you choose science, study and understand science. Whatever you choose, be sincere and practice your discipline.

Remember the human body is the most important technology ever invented. It is given to our spirit for a purpose. Develop its purpose. In the Christian faith it is the vessel to contain the Holy Spirit. In the East it is the system for facilitating the flow of Chi. Both of those definitions are the same. Energy must flow for the ingredients to work properly. Practice makes the energy flow.

Practice doesn't mean a strict, difficult physical regimen. It might if that is what you choose, but if it only meant that, then physically handicapped people would be left out.

Getting energy to flow through your body can be done in many ways. Physical exercises, visualization, prayer, all meet the criteria for opening the flow. Some work faster than others depending on the individual and the sincerity of applying the other tools. Whatever you do, you must practice diligently. Miracles do not happen by themselves. They are part of a process.

If you want to be something, be it. We don't have to wait until we do certain things in order to become what we want. Do you want to be as a saint? Act like one. To become rich, act like a rich person. Be what you want to be. This will cause you to attract the things necessary to make it your reality. Whatever you choose to be, **be it**, consistently. This is practice. At first it may seem silly or even dishonest, but eventually it will become real. If you practice.

∞∞∞∞∞∞∞∞∞∞∞∞∞∞∞∞∞∞∞

Shaky Addition

Higher vibration can come from the addition of harmonic frequencies.
When they are properly lined up they can be added.

We line them up with our greatest sensory organ.
Our heart.

The higher the vibration we attain,
The closer we are to the Source.

The closer we are to the Source,
The more we understand our own divinity.

When we are functioning as the divine within us,
We can do anything.

∞∞∞∞∞∞∞∞∞∞∞∞∞∞∞∞∞∞∞

Presence

The past is a memory, the future a wish. There is only now.

Being present means living in the moment. Being in the now. Science has proven time is a concept created by our minds. It doesn't really exist. There is no past or future. There is only now. A hard concept to grasp at first, but not impossible to understand.

Think about your past. Remember it. What is it you are doing when you think about your past? You are remembering a series of events and activities that happened in a former now. How about your future? What is that? It is a series of thoughts about what you would like things to be. Or perhaps a dread of what you think they will be. Neither is physical reality. They are thoughts.

Now is the only time there is. It is in the now that you did those things of your past. It wasn't *this* now, it was a now of the past. When you remember them, it is as if you bring the now of when they happened into the present now, which in fact is what you do. We are able to do that because we have as our memories not only the factual data surrounding a particular event, but the emotion and feeling of those facts. This is why we can remember the past, but we can't remember the future.

If we want to "remember" the future we must add the feeling and emotion to the set of facts we want to occur. That will help it to come about, or be remembered. Be like the actor: you can remember the future.

None of this happens in the past, or the future however; it can only happen now. So if you want any of this stuff to work for you in a conscious manner, you must operate in the now.

It may sound complicated and weird, but it really is very simple. We all do it, all the time. If you want to "be a singer," you must learn how to sing and you must practice. When do you do that? Now. You cannot do it any other time. You must practice now. You can think about practicing tomorrow at four o'clock, but that is not practicing. It is thinking about practicing. At four o'clock tomorrow when you are practicing, you will be practicing now, which is the only time there is.

Being present on a constant basis is not easy to do. Our heads are usually filled with many thoughts that take us somewhere else. The scholar Mihaly Csikzentmihalyi (pronounced ME-high CHEEK-sent-me-high-ee), author of *Flow*, gives us a simple exercise to help us remain in the now and enter the state he calls *flow*. Make what you are doing in the moment your goal. If you are walking across the street, make your goal a World Championship performance for walking across the street. If you are cutting your lawn, make your goal to have it be the best mowing any lawn has ever had.

If you make whatever you are doing your goal, it will cause you to focus on the moment. When you focus on the moment, you enter the flow state; you will be in the zone. This is the state where anything is possible. This will keep you in the now. The now is eternal. You will be in the eternal.

Being present is a key to being fully human. Make it a practice.

∞∞∞∞∞∞∞∞∞∞∞∞∞∞∞∞∞∞∞

Now

I choose to be here now.

I can be anywhere, in any time I want, but,
I choose to be here now.

It is easier than recovering the memory of feelings the past requires.
I choose to be here now.

Being in the future is a life of waiting.
I choose to be here now.

It is the only time anything actually happens.

∞∞∞∞∞∞∞∞∞∞∞∞∞∞∞∞∞

What we may be

"Amen, I say to you, if you have faith and do not waiver, not only will you do what has been done to the fig tree, but even if you say to this mountain, 'be lifted up and thrown into the sea,' it will be done."

The Gospel of Matthew, Chapter 21

The above quote is from Jesus Christ when asked by his disciple how he was able to curse a fig tree that didn't have any fruit for him to eat when he was hungry. Jesus put a curse on that tree so that it could never bear as much as a living leaf, let alone fruit. Needless to say, Jesus was not happy with that tree. I'm not sure what Christian doctrine says about the Son of God becoming angry at a tree or his apparent ecological shortsightedness. That is not the purpose of this writing.

It was here Jesus said we can do whatever we want. He said we can kill fig trees and move mountains at the minimum. What does that mean? Magic? Divine intervention?

What is the exact process that would kill a fig tree or move a mountain into the sea? Whatever happens in the physical, be it a miracle or a routine event, happens by a process. Some processes take a long time, like global warming. Others happen instantaneously, like lightning striking or healing a blind person simply by thinking about it. Whatever it is, it happened as a result of the ingredients spelled out here.

But Jesus didn't need to use science to do his works, you may say, he was God! Calm down brothers and sisters, it is not blasphemy to say that God allowed the sciences he created to work as he intended them. Any change that happens on the physical plane is the result of a scientific process. Even if it is initiated by a miracle.

Jesus said we could all do as he did, but he also gave us an intellect to figure it out. I don't ever remember reading anywhere of Jesus saying we must all be as the mushroom. You know what they do to mushrooms?

They keep them in the dark and feed them manure. I believe Jesus wanted us to reach our fullest potential in all aspects.

Imagine the effect on the economy, the culture, the family, the nation, the world. The entire planet would be rocked if everyone could do what Jesus said in the prior quote.

Take health care. Suppose we all were to develop the skill needed to heal ourselves. We would have no need for health insurance, doctors, nurses, pharmaceutical corporations, x-ray technicians, biological researchers, and adhesive bandage manufacturers. Even the guy who makes the blue paint used to mark handicapped parking would be out of business. Imagine how nice it would be without insurance companies being in charge of our health.

How about the loaves and fishes or the changing of water to wine. Imagine if we could multiply our food and turn our water into wine just by thinking about it. According to the Christian Bible, we can. There goes Wonder Bread and Bumblebee Tuna. Not to mention Napa Valley.

It would seem to me that many God-fearing Christians in the business community would not be keen on Christ's words coming true. It would revolutionize the business community. Entire industries would disappear. Fortunes would be lost. Movements would be created to stop the "*miracle nuts*." People would be condemned for taking Jesus' words literally.

Perhaps to some, Christ's words are nice platitudes for Sunday morning, but are not considered part of the "real" world.

∞∞∞∞∞∞∞∞∞∞∞∞∞∞∞∞∞∞∞∞

"Natural science will in time incorporate into itself the science of man, just as the science of man will incorporate into itself natural science: there will be one science."

Karl Marx, Philosopher

To those who feel themselves experts, this may seem too easy and thus rendered frivolous or fundamental. To those who think themselves logical or left brained, the sensible type, be sure this is how things happen. Try to find something that does not happen as a result of some combination of the things listed here. It will be a good exercise for your logical mind. Eventually, you will come to the same realization as I and many others. These are the ingredients for human existence.

There no doubt will be dozens of talented formal scientific minds who will determine my analysis is too simplistic, in part because it omits huge amounts of information involved in the process of making things happen, or that I made a mistake in my presentation. That is probably all true. This is not a scientific thesis; it is not written to please the academic community. It is written to move the consciousness of regular people a little bit higher. regular people do not have the time to immerse themselves in vast quantities of theoretical stuff. This will serve to open just a few minds a little bit more. That is all that is necessary for the world to change. This knowledge is like the butterfly in Lorenz' metaphor.

Eventually, these three sciences will be looked at in a deeper fashion and the realization will be forthcoming that these are three keys to the human experience which must be understood more fully. I believe these sciences will take us to an understanding of the spiritual that will remove the veils of unworthiness from our minds. Our perception will be cleansed.

When more of humanity come to a knowing that what we need is inside of us, the human experience will change. When that shift happens, an upheaval will occur. Eden will return.

∞∞∞∞∞∞∞∞∞∞∞∞∞∞∞∞∞∞∞∞∞

Many people don't like to hear it, but everything that comes into our lives is brought there by us. The first time I said that to a friend of mine he went nuts. "Are you kidding? Do you think I wanted to bring lifelong poverty into my life? There is no way I brought this to myself. Every week I buy a lottery ticket and think about nothing else except winning the big one. What you are saying is a crock!"

I didn't say he wanted lifelong poverty in his life. I know he hates being poor. But I also know he brought it. It really is about what we vibrate. If you vibrate poor, even unintentionally, you will get poor. And if you vibrate greedy pig, you will get greedy pig. No matter how you dress it up.

What about a victim of a senseless crime or the abuse of a child? What about the innocent victim of a bomb dropped or a terrorist act? Surely these can't be brought about by those people. I'm afraid they are. Perhaps a result of Chaos Mathematics with its innumerable variables at work. The butterfly didn't want to cause a tornado; it was just flapping along doing whatever butterflies do. It may have been only one of ten million variables in the equation, but necessary to bring about the exact result that occurred. And the poor butterfly may end up in the middle of the tornado. Perhaps if that butterfly had flapped its wings one less time, there would not have been a tornado.

Sure, that is really stretching the point to its furthest reaches, but it it's the way things happen. If all you think about is being poor, you will get exactly what you think about—poor. Just as the butterfly's wings attract more air, our vibrations attract similar vibrations. We get back what we put out. Like it or not.

Don't just read this book and dismiss it based on what you think you already know. Think about the tools and the technology we use to create our reality.

The things in this book are the things that every religion, every science, and every philosophy teach. It has been broken down for regular people in an easy-to-understand presentation. I didn't make up these things. Jesus said them. Buddha said them. Einstein said them. Newton said them. They all said the same thing. I am only filtering the academic and pontifical fluff away to make it more easily understood.

I suggest you read it again. In fact, read it a couple of times. It will vibrate with you as truth, and then it will become more valuable information for you.

∞∞∞∞∞∞∞∞∞∞∞∞∞∞∞∞∞∞∞∞

"In the councils of government, we must guard against the acquisition of unwarranted influence, whether sought or unsought, by the military industrial complex. The potential for the disastrous rise of misplaced power exists and will persist."

Dwight D. Eisenhower, President of the United States

We live on a planet where the entire future of the human race is in the hands of those who have the means of force at their beck and call. The rest of us are taken along for the ride. We are told the ride is the best way for everyone to prosper and have the good life. Some have the good life and don't want to rock the boat. Clearly, we can do much better.

Two ideas have been prevalent throughout our history: economics and religion. It is not my intention to present a philosophical treatise on these two concepts. But if we are going to change anything on this planet using the knowledge of how things happen, we must take a brief look at how things have happened in the past and continue to happen in our present reality. regular people have been the victims of the extremists in both of these areas. They seem to go hand in hand. We are swept up in the consequences of the plans laid out by some pretty crazy people.

Most people don't have a problem with someone making an honest buck or exercising religious freedom. The majority of people on the planet have some type of belief in a power higher than human beings. Nobody really cares, for the most part, if you choose to worship a bottle cap or your lawn mower as an incarnation of the great god "whatsisname," as long as you don't try to impose your beliefs on other people.

∞∞∞∞∞∞∞∞∞∞∞∞∞∞∞∞∞∞∞

Benito Mussolini, the creator of Fascism, defined his invention as the combining of the military with the corporation. We now have that situation. President Dwight D. Eisenhower warned us about it. The more war means profit, the more war we will get. More of our sons and daughters will die.

The cold, impersonal greed of economics has gone too far. It must be changed, just as religious fanaticism must be changed, if we are to continue here on earth. It can only change with love, the highest vibration.

∞∞∞∞∞∞∞∞∞∞∞∞∞∞∞∞∞∞

These two subjects have been interjected into this writing because they are the most potentially lethal forces on the planet if allowed to continue on their current path. Economics and religion are not the problems. It is the greed and fanaticism that have engulfed these two recipes that are the problems. If you are a regular person and are honest with yourself, you know that is the truth. We must change in order to survive.

I am not suggesting you wage a campaign to challenge these two forces. History has shown confrontation has made them consistent victors. They seem to thrive on conflict. Perhaps you may consider using the ingredients presented here to find a recipe leading to an alternative to these two running the show. This is not a suggestion to eliminate corporations and religion, as some may claim. This is a suggestion to eliminate greed and fanaticism. Things don't have to stay the way they are, unless we choose.

But imagine what it might be like if you could have the powers that Jesus said you could.

∞∞∞∞∞∞∞∞∞∞∞∞∞∞∞∞∞∞

Whatever recipe you choose to fulfill your destiny, these are the ingredients:

Quantum Physics
Morphic Resonance
Chaos Mathematics
The Human Body
Thought
Emotions
Feelings
Beliefs
Intentions
Allowing
Energy

These are the things that make things happen. These are your ingredients. You can use them in any recipe you choose. Now that you know them, your life will change.

Even if you don't believe anything you have read here, your life will change. Perhaps only by the new mental defenses you deploy.

There is one thing to use as a measurement for any recipe you choose to help you live your life. If it doesn't allow for your freedom in all regards, it is not the truth. Try another.

Be well.

∞∞∞∞∞∞∞∞∞∞∞∞∞∞∞∞∞

Metamorphosis

Caterpillars are lucky. They get to sleep through the changes.
They don't know what happened.
They don't know they are beautiful.

Butterflies are probably too amazed at the aerial view to think about
themselves.
Of course caterpillars and butterflies are not known to be great thinkers.

We humans on the other hand get to experience every emotion at various
amplitudes as we pass from one level to the next.

Humans are more fortunate. It may not always
be comfortable but,
We get to call our own game.

We get to watch the changes happen before our eyes.
We feel them. We live them.

You don't have to be a butterfly.
You can be whatever you wish.
It isn't about luck,
*We **want** it this way.*
From now on,
I choose to be a sincere human being.
Thank You God.

∞∞∞∞∞∞∞∞∞∞∞∞∞∞∞∞∞∞∞

About the Author

Bill Kane is the past President of the New Jersey Industrial Union Council and former New Jersey Area Director of the Auto Workers Union. He has served on many boards, commissions, and committees in the private, public, and academic sectors.

A lifelong student of human potential and science, Kane has also practiced several martial and healing arts, including Tae Kwan Do, Aikido, Dahn Hak, and Universal Tao Inner Alchemy practices.

Bill lives in Westwood, New Jersey. He can be reached at bill@regularpeoplesplace.com.

∞∞∞∞∞∞∞∞∞∞∞∞∞∞∞∞∞∞∞∞∞∞